Volleyball

Bernie Blackall

Special thanks to Allan Rubenstein, Men's Volleyball Coach, Rollins College

Heinemann Library
Des Plaines, Illinois

First published in the United States by Heinemann Library,
an imprint of Reed Educational & Professional Publishing,
1350 East Touhy Avenue, Suite 240 West
Des Plaines, IL 60018

© Bernie Blackall 1998

02 01 00 99 98
10 9 8 7 6 5 4 3 2 1

Series cover and text design by Karen Young
Paged by Jo Pritchard
Cover by Smarty-pants Design
Cover photographs by: Sport. The Library/Jeff Crow (left); Mike Liles
Edited by Jane Pearson
Illustrations by Vasja Komen
Picture research by Kirsty Grant and Lara Artis
Production by Cindy Smith
Film separations by Impact Printing Pty Ltd
Printed in Hong Kong by Wing King Tong

Library of Congress Cataloging-in-Publication Data

Blackall, Bernie, 1956-
    Volleyball / Bernie Blackall.
        p.   cm. -- (Top Sport)
    Includes bibliographical references (p.) and index.
    Summary: Introduces volleyball, discussing its history, American
    highlights, skills, rules, equipment, and events.
    ISBN 1-57572-706-4 (lib. bdg.)
    1. Volleyball--Juvenile literature. [1. Volleyball.] I. Title.
    II. Series: Blackall, Bernie, 1956- Top sport.
    GV1015.3.B53   1998
    796.325--dc21   98-19591
                                                            CIP
                                                             AC

Acknowledgements
The publisher would like to thank:
Craig Smith, Head coach, Victorian Institute of Sport,
Simone Brown, Narelle Lloyd and Peter Jones of Volleyball Victoria,
Ana Paulic, Australian Volleyball Federation., Greg Tossie and Whitney Tossie

Photographs supplied by:
Coo-ee Picture Library: pp. 11 (top), 20. Mike Liles: pp. 11 (bottom), 19 (top), 23 (left). Sporting Pix: Greg Ford, p. 26; Bob Thomas, p. 17. Jeff Crow pp. 14, 23 (right); Andrew Freeman p. 27. Sydney Freelance: pp. 5, 10, 19 (bottom). Volleyball Hall of Fame, Holyoke, Massachusetts: p 8. YMCA of the USA Archives, University of Minnesota Libraries: p. 9; Allsport/Susan Allen Sigmon, p. 6; Allsport/Don Liebig, p.7.

Some words are shown in bold, **like this.** You can find out what they mean by looking in the glossary.

Volleyball requires special instruction. Do not attempt any of the techniques and movements in this book without a qualified, registered instructor present.

Contents

About Volleyball

Volleyball is an Olympic sport with an estimated 250 million players worldwide. It is a team game played on a **court** divided by a high net. There are six players per team, and each team aims to hit the ball over the net to land on its opponent's court.

Play begins with the ball being **served** by a **back court** player who stands behind the back boundary line, called the **end line,** of the court. After the ball is served over the net, each team is allowed three touches before the ball is hit back over the net. They must not let the ball touch the ground on their side of the court, or they will give the other team a point or lose the serve.

Only the serving team can score a point. When the serving team wins a **rally**, a point is added to its score, and the team continues to **serve**. When the receiving team wins a rally, there is no change to the score, but it wins the right to serve. This is called a side-out.

A **set** is won by the first team to score 15 points—as long as the team has a two-point lead. The match winner is the first team to win three sets.

Played at top level, volleyball is a very dynamic and spectacular sport.

With the official introduction of beach volleyball at the 1996 Olympic Games, a new dimension has been added to the game. Rules have been modified for the new two-player-per-side format.

U.S. Highlights

Although volleyball started out as a recreational sport, over the past several years, it has grown on popularity as a competitive sport as well. USA Volleyball, the governing organization for volleyball in the United States reports that there are between 1,100 and 1,200 junior volleyball clubs nationwide. There are also some highly competitive leagues at the junior level.

Laura Davis

Laura Davis plays on the U.S. National Women's Volleyball team. Like most athletes, her's is a story of determination and persistence. Throughout her career she's had to rely on her self-determination at a shorter than average height of 5-foot-7 where most of her teammates are around 6-feet tall. She was a star on the volleyball team in high school. Her coach was discouraging when she said she was going to get a volleyball scholarship to college. She did just that. She

Laura Davis in action with a dig

attended Ohio State on a full scholarship and earned the 1994 AVCA Division I Player of the Year and the Big Ten Player of the Year awards. She hopes to play in the Olympics in Sydney in 2000.

Ethan Watts

Ethan Watts is a rising talent in volleyball. Born in Tulsa, Oklahoma in 1974, he attended Brigham Young University where he played four years of varsity volleyball. He made the first-team All-America in his senior year (1994) and NCAA second-team All-America as a junior (1993). He made the NCAA all-freshman team in 1991 and was on the Athletic Honor Roll. During his senior year of high school he played club volleyball. and he also participated in wrestling and football. He joined the U.S. National team in 1994 at the age of 22 and played on the U.S. Men's Olympic Volleyball team in Atlanta in 1996. Currently he is living in Italy and playing for a top team there and one of the best in the world. He hopes this experience will make him an even better player as he looks forward to returning to the U.S. team.

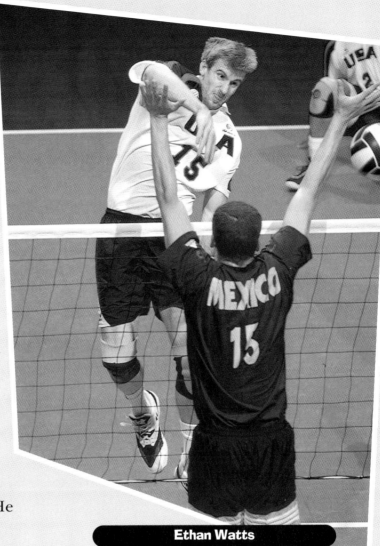

Ethan Watts

U.S. Olympic Beach Volleyball

In the 1996 Olympics in Atlanta, Beach Volleyball was a competitive sport for the first time. U.S. Men's teams won both the gold and the silver medals. Winning the gold were Karsh Kirally and Kent Steffes. The silver went to Mike Dodd and Mike Whitmarsh. Kent Steffes and Karsh Kirally have been playing volleyball as a team since 1991. They've won over 50 competitions.

History of Volleyball

The original Holyoke volleyball team. William Morgan is standing at the left.

Mintonette

Morgan adapted the rules and the equipment from several games already in existence. From tennis he borrowed the net and strung it at a height of 7 feet (2 meters) across the middle of a basketball court. He used the bladder of a basketball as it was soft and light, allowing players to volley the ball without pain or injury. Morgan's new game was called mintonette.

The basic rule of mintonette was that the ball must not touch the ground. A point was scored to the opposition when it did. Players were required to volley the ball back over the net—they were not allowed to catch it. Teams consisted of nine players each set in three rows of three. Team **rotation** on the court ensured that all players took turns in all positions on the court during a game.

Volleyball originated in Holyoke, Massachusetts, in 1895. William G. Morgan, a young instructor at the Young Men's Christian Association (YMCA), had introduced basketball to his middle-aged members but they found it too fast and too demanding.

He decided to create a game that involved less running and that could be played in a smaller area.

Volleyball was a popular outdoor game. This game is being played in Maryland in 1911.

A new name

At the YMCA conference in 1896, the name volleyball was adopted because every hit was a **volley**. Teams were reduced to six players, the court was enlarged slightly and a new, lighter leather ball was introduced.

Volleyball spread quickly throughout the United States—largely through the YMCA network. In 1918 the game was introduced into Western Europe by American troops. From here it spread around the world. It became highly popular in Japan and Russia—countries that still dominate international competition.

In Paris in 1947 the International Volleyball Federation (Federatione Internationale de Volleyball—FIVB) was formed. It remains the sport's governing body. The first World Championships for men were held in 1949 and for women in 1952. Since 1962 these championships have been held every four years.

An Olympic sport

Volleyball became an Olympic sport at the Tokyo Olympics in 1964. At the Olympic level, the men's gold medallists were Netherlands 1996 and Brazil 1992. Women's Olympic events have been dominated by Cuba.

What You Need to Play

The court

A volleyball match is usually played indoors on a wooden floor court measuring 60x30 feet (18x9 meters). The 2-inch (50-millimeter) wide boundary lines mark the edges of the court—any balls that hit the lines are considered "in." The court is divided into two equal sections by the **center line**.

Above the center line is the net, which is about 3 feet (1 meter) in depth and varies in height depending upon the age and gender of the players. The official height of the net, measured at its midpoint, is 7 feet 4 inches (2.24 meters) for women and 7 feet 11 inches (2.43 meters) for men. However, the net height can be reduced for skills practice. For all but official games, the net height does not need to be precise.

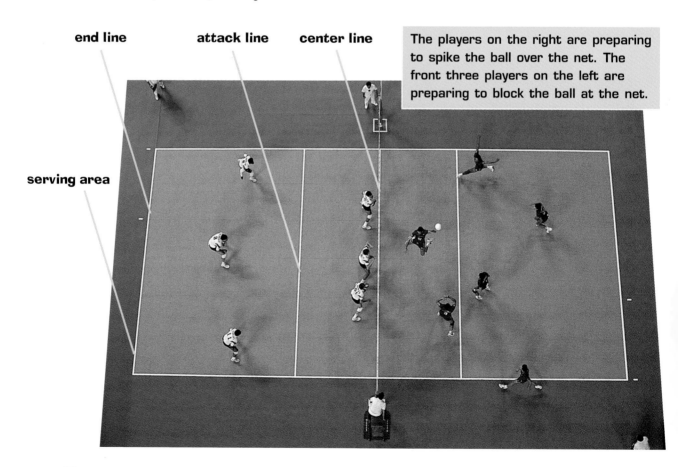

end line   attack line   center line

serving area

The players on the right are preparing to spike the ball over the net. The front three players on the left are preparing to block the ball at the net.

Volleyball can be played on outdoor courts.

Across each half of the court, there is an attack line located 10 feet (3 meters) from the net.

The attack line divides each side of the court into a front zone (the **attack zone**) and a back zone. Only the three front-court players on each team are permitted to spike the ball from within the attack zone. (Players from the back court may enter the attacking zone, but they may not play the ball from above the height of the net.)

The volleyball

The official volleyball is a light color, although outdoor balls may be colored, and 25 to 26 inches (65 to 67 centimeters) in circumference. Modified volleyballs are available for younger players. These softer balls are ideal for beginners as they allow the players to develop good handling techniques.

Clothing and shoes

Volleyball is played in shorts and a loose-fitting T-shirt. In competitions players on a team must all wear the same color.

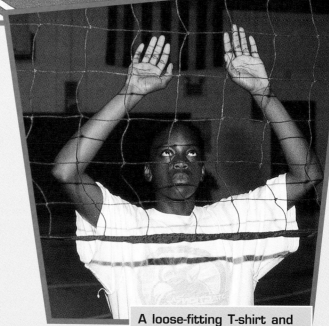

A loose-fitting T-shirt and shorts are fine for playing volleyball.

An all-purpose sports shoe is ideal for the beginner to intermediate-level player. A thick sole (to provide cushioning) should provide a good grip. The sole must be nonmarking for indoor courts.

Knee pads

Because players often **dive** for low balls, knee pads allow the player to play these balls with a reduced risk of knee injury.

Rules

The object of the game of volleyball is to play the ball over the net and into the opponent's court by using any part of the body. Intentional contacts with the ball below the knee are not legal indoors but are permitted outdoors. The ball must never caught or held. Each team tries to play shots that their opponents will be unable to return.

A team may contact the ball three times before it travels back over the net.

Playing the ball

Each contact must give the ball immediate flight. The ball must be hit cleanly—it may not be **carried** (held for any length of time), lifted, scooped, or thrown. The ball may be contacted with one hand or two, or any part of the body.

The block does not count as a contact.

The three-contact rule

A **contact** occurs whenever the ball touches a team member. Before returning the ball over the net, a team may contact the ball a maximum of three times. A fourth contact would result in a point to the other team or loss of service for the offending team. The ball may be legally hit back over the net with fewer than three contacts.

The only exception to the "three-contact rule" occurs when a **block** at the net rebounds into the team's court. A block is a shot that attempts to stop a ball coming over the net. The player jumps up at the net with both hands up to block the ball as it is **spiked** or attacked across the net by a player on the other side. The block is not counted as a contact so the team is still allowed its three contacts. However, a block does count as a contact in outdoor or beach volleyball.

Double hit

A **double hit** is legal on the *first* contact or when the player first blocks the ball and then plays the ball again without a teammate touching it. A double hit occurs when a player touches the ball twice in succession on his or her side of the net.

Rules

Serving

Before the match begins, the captains toss a coin for choice of "side or **serve**." The winning captain can choose to serve or to start the game from a preferred side of the court.

The player to begin serving stands behind the **end line**. The umpire blows a whistle, and the server has 5 seconds to play the ball. It is legal to serve underhand or overhand, provided the ball is struck cleanly with one hand only. The ball must be tossed into the air prior to being struck by the serving hand.

The serving player must:
- stand behind the end line.
- strike the ball cleanly over the net, without touching the net.
- strike the ball so that it does not contact any of the server's team prior to its flight over the net. Only one attempt at service is allowed. If a serve is not successful, there is no change made to the score, but the opposing team is awarded the service.
- strike the ball so that it doesn't land outside the opponent's court.

Attackers and blockers can extend their arms over the net as they play their shots.

Winning a point

A team wins a point when it has the service, and the other team makes an error. These include:
- allowing the ball to touch the ground inside the court or on the boundary lines
- touching the ball more than the three permitted times before sending it back over the net
- hitting the ball over the net so that it lands on the other side, but outside the opponent's court
- touching the net
- rule violations (double hits, lifts, etc.)

Touching the opponent's court

No part of the body may completely cross the center line to touch the opposite court. Your foot or hand may touch your opponent's court, but some part of it must stay in contact with the center line.

Touching the net

The ball may not touch the net on service, but once the rally is in progress, it is permitted to touch the net while crossing it. If the ball rebounds off the net, it may be played again only if the team has not already used its three contacts.

When a player's body or clothing touches the net, a violation occurs. It is also illegal to pass the hand over the net to play a shot, unless the player is blocking a **spike**.

Ball in and out of bounds

The ball is "in" if it lands anywhere on the court, including on any of the boundary lines. Even if the ball only touches the line slightly it is considered to be "in."

The ball is "out" if it lands outside the court without touching the boundary lines, or if it touches the ceiling or an object outside the court.

It is also "out" if it hits the net without passing over it. If a ball is "out," your opponents will score a point or your team will lose the service, depending on which team served the rally.

Substitutions

Each team may have up to 6 substitute players. Each team is permitted 12 substitutions in each set, with each player entering the game a maximum of three times. A rule modification in 1998/99 allows teams 15 *total* substitutions with no limit on a player going into the game.

A player's foot may only cross the center line into the opponent's court if some part of the foot is on the line.

Rules

Player positions

The teams spread themselves across the court so that the entire court is covered. The "W formation" is usually used for receiving serve as it gives excellent coverage of the court.

- The center front player (CF) stays at the net facing his teammates.
- The center back player (CB) stands in the center of the back court.
- The front-court players (RF and LF) cover the wide areas at mid-court.
- The right and left back players (RB and LB) cover their respective back corners.

Scoring

Three or five sets are played in a volleyball match (two out of three for high school). The winner is the team that wins the most sets.

When one team has won 15 points they have won a set—but they must have a lead of at least two points. If a game reaches a score of 14–14, play continues until one team gains a two-point lead or reaches 17 points. At the end of each set, teams change ends.

Serving team

Receiving team

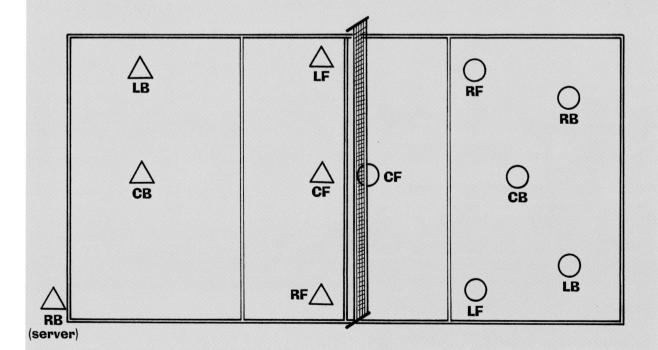

Officials

A competition match is controlled by two officials. The referee, who is in charge of the game, stands on a platform at the center of the net. He decides whether a ball has been played legally, and when to award a point or a side-out (change of service).

The umpire stands at ground level opposite the referee. He or she controls substitutions, timeouts, **rotations,** and net offenses.

Line judges assist the referee and the umpire to determine whether balls land in or outside the court.

Beginner-level matches are usually controlled by one umpire.

The attack zone

Once the ball is in play, the players may move around the court. However, the three back-court players are restricted in how they can play if they move into the attack zone (the front 10 feet [3 meters] of the court). When a **back court** player moves into the front court, he or she must not play the ball while it is above the height of the top of the net. In most cases this restricts these players to nonattacking shots in the front court.

Rotation

During a game each player will play in each of the six positions. The players rotate one position when the team regains the serve. While a team continues to win rallies, the same server continues to serve and the players stay in their positions. When the team loses a rally, a side-out occurs—the opponents take over the serve.

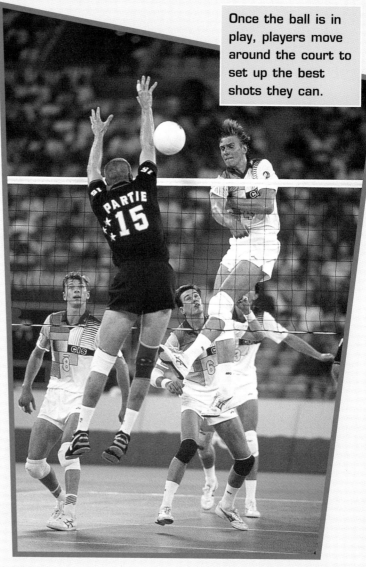

Once the ball is in play, players move around the court to set up the best shots they can.

The players of the new serving team rotate one position in a clockwise direction (facing the net). The player who was in the right front (RF) position now takes the ball to serve.

Change of ends

Teams change ends after each set. They have a 3-minute break between sets. If the match is taken to a fifth set, a coin is tossed to determine which team will serve first and from which end each team will play. In the fifth deciding set, the teams change ends when one of them reaches eight points.

Skills

There are two main areas of skills to learn to become a good volleyball player: serving and **passing** the ball. There are three **serves** and three main ways to pass the ball.

Serving:
• the underhand serve
• the overhand serve
• the **jump serve**

Passing the ball:
• the **dig**
• the **set**
• the **spike**

Serving

A serve begins each rally. With just one chance to serve the ball correctly, it is important to learn and practice this skill.

Underhand serve

Stand side-on to the net with your feet shoulder-width apart. Support the ball with your **platform hand**, the one closest to the net. Make a fist as you take your hitting hand back.

Move your weight to your front foot as you swing your hitting hand through. Drop your platform hand away from the ball just before striking it. Make contact with the ball in front of you at about waist height.

Hit the ball with the base of the palm of your hand. The ball should be at about waist height when you hit it. Follow through toward your target.

Underhand serve

The underhand serve should be mastered first. The ball travels over the net and into the opposite court in a high curve. It is an accurate and safe serve. The rules state that the ball must be hit cleanly with one hand only so be careful to keep your platform hand clear of the volleyball when your striking hand makes contact.

Overhand serve

The overhand serve is a powerful serve that puts the opponent under immediate pressure. Stand facing the net with one foot slightly forward.

Make a fist as you take your arm straight back for the underhand serve.

As you throw the ball up, bring your contact hand back behind your shoulder. Swing it powerfully forward as you step onto your front foot and hit the ball with a firm open hand.

Jump serve

The jump serve is an overhand serve where the server jumps up to strike the ball overhead while airborne. It can be used to give the serve more power, but should be played only when you have mastered the overhand serve.

The overhand serve action is similar in motion to the tennis serve.

Skills

Passing the ball

Passing the ball from one teammate to another can be made with either a **dig** or a **set.**

Dig

The dig is normally used when receiving the ball from an attack or service. The aim is to let the ball bounce cleanly on your forearms so that it travels in a high curve to a player at the front of the court.

As the ball approaches, move quickly to a position behind it with your knees bent and feet shoulder-width apart. Aim to contact the ball at or below waist level. For a low ball, bend your knees low to get down under it.

Place your arms so that the ball strikes your forearms just above the wrists. Bend your legs to absorb some of the ball's force to help you control its path. Straighten your legs after the ball bounces and follow through with your arms to about chin height.

Place the fingers of one hand across the fingers of your other and put your thumbs together. Contact is made with the forearms. A flat surface is essential as the ball is then unlikely to bounce off to the side.

With his knees bent and arms straight, this player is well-prepared to dig the ball safely to a teammate.

Set

The set is played when the ball approaches from above head height. Its most common use is to set up for an attacking spike, but it is also ideal to send the ball long and high into an opponent's back court. It is generally the second shot in the three-contact sequence of play (see page 13).

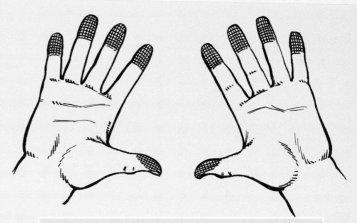

Contact with the ball should be made just above the forehead with the fingers of both hands cupped around and under the ball.

Move quickly into position with one leg in front of the other and your knees bent.

Bend your arms with your elbows outward as you extend your hands above your head.

Straighten your legs and arms as you flick your wrists to power the ball away.

Skills

Spike

Sometimes called the smash, the **spike** is the most dynamic and attacking of all volleyball shots. Your aim is to smash the ball down hard into the opposite court. The spike is played from a position close to the net when the ball is high, usually when a teammate has positioned it with a set.

Block

Most volleyball shots are attacking shots with the aim of setting up or executing winning shots. The **block,** however, is used to defend against the powerful spike. If players notice that their opponents are setting up a spike, they can prepare to defend by being ready to block the ball as it is hit down hard across the net.

When the ball is high and close to the net, jump as high as you can.

With an arm action like a tennis serve, strike the ball from above net height with a firm, cupped hand. Aim to project the ball down hard and fast into your opponent's court.

From a crouched position push off vertically with both feet. Your timing must be perfect, something achieved only with lots of practice.

An effective block turns a threatening spike into an attacking shot—possibly a point-winning shot.

The block is performed with both arms up, less than a ball-width apart, and your fingers spread to maximize the area used to block the ball. Sometimes a block can send the ball straight back to the opponent's side of the net. Other times it can deflect the ball over the player's head to his or her teammates.

Dive

The dive can be used to **save** a very difficult ball. It is used when the ball is wide and out of range of the dig and involves diving for the ball to save it from bouncing. Once you have saved the ball, a teammate can then keep it in play.

Push off one foot and jump or dive horizontally toward the ball. Play the ball from your forearm before landing. Once you have played the dive, move quickly back into position.

Skills

Teamwork

As well as practicing the individual shots used in volleyball, it is important to practice sequences with your team. The usual sequence for the three contacts your team may have with the ball before it is sent back over the net is **dig, pass, set, spike.**

The dig takes the force out of the ball as it is received from the opposing team and sends it high in the air towards the net.

The set receives the ball from the dig and springs it into the air close to the net, setting up the final contact.

1. The ball is hit over the net.

2. The ball is received with a dig that takes the speed off the ball and directs it to the attack zone at the front of the court.

3. The set puts the ball in the attacking zone within about 3 feet (1 meter) of the net.

4. The ball is spiked by a leaping player who uses a powerful striking action to smash the ball over the net.

5. With outstretched arms and hands, a player on the opposing team tries to block the ball.

6. When the block is unsuccessful a teammate may be able to dive to dig the ball up and back into play.

The spike powerfully smashes the ball into the opponent's court. It might be met with a block or a dig, or it may hit the court resulting in a point for your team or a side-out, giving your team the serve.

If you are playing a dig, it is important to try to send the ball towards a player who is well positioned to play a good set. Likewise, if you are playing a set, be aware of the player who will jump up to spike the ball. Plenty of practice with your teammates will help you to anticipate where their shots will be placed and to know where best to place yours.

This sequence allows for a strong attacking shot to be played over the net to your opponents. However it is not compulsory to play a spike over the net. Until you are confident with the spike, the set can be played over the net.

Rallys

In a rally, the ball passes back and forth over the net any number of times before play is stopped by the ball hitting the ground or the net, or by illegal play. The illustration below shows a typical sequence of shots in a rally.

Beach Volleyball

Beach volleyball has been an Olympic sport since the 1996 Olympic Games in Atlanta. It was first played on the beaches of southern California in the 1920s. Originally it was played in the traditional six-a-side format, but it was modified to a four-a-side game and then to the two-a-side game that it is today.

As the popularity of beach volleyball grew, the International Volleyball Federation promoted the World Beach Series, the World Indoor League, and the European Grand Prix.

Rules

The rules of the standard game of volleyball have been adapted for the two-a-side beach game. The differences are:

- there are two players per team
- the ball is slightly heavier but softer, making it easier to control and less affected by the wind

Players usually wear swimwear, often with hats and sunglasses, and they usually play in bare feet.

- the game is played on sand
- there is no attack line and so no distinction between front court and **back court** players
- there is no **center line** and players are allowed under the net as long as they don't interfere with their opponents
- teams change ends after every five points instead of after every **set**
- the court is the same size as for the standard game
- the boundary of the court is marked with ropes. The corners of the boundary are secured with anchors buried in the sand.
- the two players may stand anywhere on the court. Unlike the standard game of volleyball, players are not restricted to certain positions at the moment of service. When receiving a **spike,** one player usually stands ready to **block** at the net, while the other covers the rest of the court. When receiving **serve,** each player stands in the back third of the court.
- players follow the rule of rotation as each player takes a turn at serving
- the ball may be held slightly when

Beach volleyball is a popular summertime sport.

setting, especially when it is being played from a difficult position or from a hard-hit attack
- a block shot is included as one of the team's three permitted contacts
- the service may be received and played only with a **dig.** You may use your hands in a setting fashion but cannot carry the ball. The second hit is then used to set up your teammate for the spike.

Getting Ready

Always warm up your body before a match or practice session to minimize the risk of injury. Begin with running or jogging for a few minutes and then perform the stretches below.

Repeat each exercise four times on each side of the body. Hold each stretch for between 10 and 15 seconds and then relax the muscles before the next exercise.

Shoulder stretch
Stretch one arm straight across your body. Use your other hand to pull your elbow in to your chest until you feel the stretch.

Lower back stretch
Lie on your back with your legs outstretched. Bend one knee up to your chest and lift your head and shoulders off the floor to meet it. Lower yourself slowly back to the floor.

Arm and shoulder stretch
Bend your arm behind your head and gently push your elbow down with your other hand.

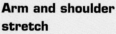

Inner thigh stretch
Stand with your feet wide apart and your toes pointing forwards. Rest your hands on one thigh and bend that knee. Keep your back straight and lean into your knee until you feel the stretch.

Arm circles
Stretch your arms above your head and then take them around in circles forwards and then backwards, stretching as far up and around as you can.

Calf stretch
Stand with one foot about 3 feet (1 meter) in front of the other. Bend your leading leg and lean forward, keeping both feet flat on the floor.

Quadricep stretch
Hold a wall, beam, or a partner with one hand for balance. Bend one knee and pull your foot up behind you.

Side bends
Stand upright with one hand on your waist. Bring your other hand up over your head as you bend to the side. Make sure you don't lean forward as you bend.

Taking it Further

USA

USA Volleyball
3595 E. Fountain Blvd.
Suite 1-2
Colorado Springs, CO 80910-1740
☎ (719) 637-8300

USA Volleyball
Outdoor Committee Chairman
Dr. Neal Luebke
8010 Continental Drive
Brookfield, WI 53045-1204
☎ (414) 781-6502

Association of Volleyball
Professionals (AVP)
330 Washington Blvd.
Suite 600
Marina Del Rey, CA 90292
☎ (310) 577-0775

More Books to Read

Burby, Liza N. Gabrielle Reece, *Star Volleyball Player*. New York: Rosen Publishing Group, 1997.

Costanzo, Christie. *Volleyball*. Vero Beach, FL: Rourke Corporation. 1993.

Jensen, Julie. *Beginning Volleyball*. Minneapolis, MN: The Lerner Publishing Group, 1995.

Glossary

attack line line dividing each side of the court into the attack zone and the back court. It is 10 feet from the center line and parallel to it.

attack zone area of the court between the net and the attack line

back court the back 20 feet of the volleyball court

block a defensive move to prevent an attacking ball from coming over the net

carrying catching a ball, however slightly, before sending it up and back into play

center line the line directly under the net that divides the court in two

contact whenever a player touches the ball

court the net, the boundary lines, and the playing area

dig to recover a low ball by playing it with both your forearms under the ball.

dive a recovery of the ball when it is very low by diving onto the court to get beneath it

double hit illegally hitting the ball twice in succession

end line the back boundary line of the court called the serve line

jump serve an overhead serve in which the server strikes the ball while airborne

passing sending the ball from one teammate to another

platform hand hand holding the ball just prior to service

rally a sequence of play in which the ball passes back and forth over the net several times before a point is scored

rotation each player moves clockwise to the next position when their team gains service

save preventing a low ball from hitting the court

serve to bring the ball into play at the start of each new rally. The serve is hit directly over the net from behind the end line.

set a play to set the ball up for the spiker to spike it over the net. The set is played with the fingertips.

set (game) part of a match. A set is won when one team reaches 15 points.

side-out change of service. When the team receiving serve wins a rally, they don't add a point to their score, but they gain service.

spike a powerful attacking shot where the ball is forcefully hit down across the net

volley a shot where the ball is played before it bounces. In volleyball, every legal shot is a volley.

Index